Horns, Claws and Whiskers

Preface

This little book began life as a bit of fun back in the 1970s when Carol [Who painted the wonderful Illustrations], friend Patsy, and I shared a flat together for a few years after leaving college.

Jobs and marriage took us in separate ways many years ago, but we have remained good friends, seeing each other often. We returned to this project off and on over the years, much to the frustration of Patsy, who has been assiduous in reminding us regularly to "Get the book finished"!

Now we have all retired, we seem to have finally got there, and would like to dedicate this to our husbands and friends who have had to put up with our dithering.

Our especial thanks to James, whose technological talent and hard work have enabled us to get our little book published.

Lion

Velvet paws and golden mane
Lion lazes on the plain
Predator in his domain
Harem at his side.

Flexes his enormous claws
Stretches out and opens jaws
Takes a breath, and then he ROARS!
Master of his pride.

Hare

With a flash of grey fur and in ecstasy wild
The hare dances madly in Spring.
With paws in the air, he boxes and leaps
For the joys that the summer will bring.

Through dappled green fields and new shoots of corn
The hare tumbles over the slope.
In the gold of the sun he then flings himself high
To welcome the season of hope.

Warthog

Oh, hark to the song of the warthog
While through the forest I grunt
Turning each leaf and each dry log
As for some insects I hunt.

You may think that I'm not a beauty
But why over looks make a fuss?
To eat is our primary duty
And sufficient for creatures like us.

My unprepossessing appearance
May cause you to give me a snub
But a tough hide will soon make a clearance
In the thickest and prickliest scrub.

My tusks may look awe-inspiring
But no need to scuttle from me.
Can't you see I'm already perspiring
Inspecting the roots of this tree?

So remember the song of the warthog
If ever you meet me one day.
I'm happy in ditch, dyke or deep bog,
And I'll thank you to leave me that way.

Cats

They love to snooze in sunshine, they curl up on your chair
They'll ooze in through an open door, they turn up everywhere.
All gardens are their playground, they *know* they own your house
And to show appreciation, they'll offer you a mouse.
The felines of this world turn up in many shapes and sizes;
Consider cats in literature - they offer some surprises.
The cats of Mr Elliot were numerous and clever
Magical, mysterious, purr-fect in each endeavour.
Mr. Seuss's wore a hat in a book with simple rhymes
And Lewis Carroll's Cheshire cat could vanish many times.
Lear's pussycat who wed an owl was another funny creature.
While some of Beatrix Potter's tales had cats as their main feature
Kipling's cat walked by himself, all places were the same.
But whether real or fictional, no cat is truly tame
They can be large and predatory, or can be small and cute
Whatever shape or size they are, they're graceful and astute.
They can be fierce and fearsome, or fluffy little friskers,
They *all* know they're adorable, in fact, they're the CATS WHISKERS.

Bats

Bats in the belfry,
Bats in the barn;
Flitting through the darkness,
Never do us harm.
Pipistrelle or Horseshoe,
Black bat or brown
Feeding on the insects
In the field or town.
Echolocation- -
Clever little things;
Doing us a favour -
Pest control on wings!

Platypus

"Oh wisest of creatures, Madam Platypus,
We're begging you to join our group, you must be one of us.
Fine eggs you lay, and have a bill as fine as any bird;
To think of you in any other group would be absurd.
Won't you come and join us now? You'd fill us all with pride."
"I'll go away and think about it," Platypus replied.

"Oh wisest of creatures, Madam Platypus,
We think that you are more like fish, you should be one of us.
Your underwater swimming is both elegant and swift
You move through water just like us, it really is a gift!
What's your answer? Won't you come and join the fish's side?
I'll go away and think about it," Platypus replied.

"Oh wisest of creatures, Madam Platypus.
You surely are a mammal, of course you're one of us!
You have a sleek and furry coat, and like us, you breathe air,
Your tail is like a beaver's, and your growl is like a bear.
You'll never find a better group, however hard you tried."
"I'll go away and think about it," Platypus replied.

So Platypus, she went away and thought both hard and long
About the group of animals to which she should belong.
"I know that I'm a mammal, despite the eggs I lay,
So in some ways I'm like a bird, at least that's what they say.
And yet the fishes want me too, because I like to swim.
They've put me in a proper state; to make a choice is grim!"

This wisest of animals quite soon made up her mind
And called together all the many creatures she could find.
"I really am most flattered," she began, as they sat down,
"That you think my being in your group would bring you great renown.
But I belong with all of you, and yet again, with none;
We each of us is different, but together live as one."
"Oh Platypus, how wise you are!" the animals all cried.
"Just go away and think about it," Platypus replied.

The Platypus then nodded to them all, and turned her bill,
And went back to her river, which is where you'll find her still.

[From "The Dreaming" – Australian Aboriginal creation stories]

Tortoise

A lump of earth was on the grass
"Who put that there?" I cried.
"I mow that lawn each bloomin' week
No wonder that I chide!
I keep this garden spick and span
And now this lump appears.
I'll bet it is some rotten mole:
It moves me quite to tears."
All at once, the "lump" stood up;
A little head looked round.
It gave me quite a sorry look,
As if some fool he'd found.
Then little legs began to move
And with air most mortified
The tortoise moved towards the hedge
With sorely wounded pride.

Sloth

The three-toed sloth
Is loth
To put one foot before another.
The will to move
Can prove
To be a nuisance and a bother.
His shady tree,
We see
Is perfect for his three-clawed feet.
With sleepy eyes
He tries
To focus on the need to eat.
A piece of fruit
A shoot
A leaf or two to keep him going.
His fur is seen
As green
Because of algae on him growing.
He hides away
All day
Looking like the vegetation.
This hairy mutt
Is but
A poor excuse for animation.

Bull

A bull stood in his field one day
And pondered on his life.
"There's something missing here" he thought,
"Perhaps I need a wife".

And so he lumbered to the gate
As bulls so often do,
He took himself by both his horns
And smashed his way right through.

In new found freedom he set off:
His quest he had to start,
With nostrils flared and gleaming eye
And romance in his heart.

A little way along the lane
A field of cows he spied,
And one stood out from all the rest:
All brown and dewy–eyed.

Our bull fell instantly in love,
And bashfully he said,
"How now, brown cow? – My heart is yours;
I yearn for us to wed!"

She sidled up towards the fence
And coyly she did glance.
"This is so sudden sir", she said,
"But I'll give love a chance".

In just a trice, the fence was down;
They romped through grass and heather.
And from that day they went their way
To chew the cud together.

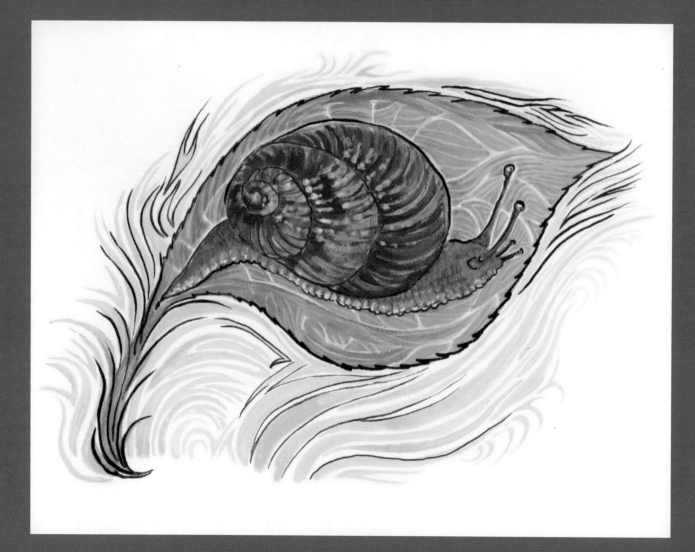

Snail

The snail doth set a ponderous pace
It's slow but sure that wins the race.
But will he become the snails' Wells Fargo
Or simply end up on the plate as Escargot?

Puffins reunited

Well, my dear, it's been a year,
And now we're back together.
You haven't changed a bit, my dear,
Not a single feather!
Your orange feet are oh so neat,
Your bill is sharp and red.

Your feathers gleam, your eyes are
bright,
So black and white your head!"
And now, my pet, we are all set:
Our burrow's dry and deep.
Our precious egg's about to hatch-
Just hear our puffling cheep!"

A cracking egg, a beak, a leg
The chick is now emerging;
And now he's here, he must be fed
His parents need no urging.

With whirring wing, the puffins fling
Themselves into the ocean.
Acrobats beneath the waves
Poetry in motion.

A herring meal, or fresh sandeel
Are brought with feathers ruffling;
Their fishing skills put to the test
To feed their little puffling!

"We're ocean's clown in motley gown
As birds we lack perfection,
Yet Arctic snows and iceberg floes
Cause us no introspection.
We flap, we fly 'twixt sea and sky
In avian elation."

Parrot of the sea, you are unique
Endearing puffination!

Spider

I spied a spider on the wall,
She wasn't doing much at all.
Sleepy, quiet, clinging there;
I sauntered by without a care.
What's this?
A sticky web!
A snare!
No one noticed my shrill cry,
For I was simply one more fly.

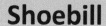

Shoebill

In the continent of Africa, far from the homes of Man,

Standing like a statue in the swamps of the Sudan

A bird of vast proportions in a feathered coat of grey

Is waiting very patiently to spot his fishy prey

A lightning strike, a fish is caught, his aim is often true,

And many fish can well be held in a bill shaped like a shoe.

Some see this bird as comical, an avian disgrace,

But it's hard to maintain dignity with footwear on your face.

Zebra

They say that creatures all have coats
To suit their clime or nature:
The polar bear has thick white hair
To thwart the temperature
The porcupines have long sharp spines
To ward off friend or foe,
And chameleons can change their hue
So that their skins won't show.

The crocodile may smugly grin,
Their coats are waterproof
The tortoise goes from tail to nose
Beneath his private roof.
A shaggy hide is worn with pride
By South American Llamas
But, rain or shine, come day or night,
The zebra wears pyjamas.

Fiddler Crab

From the quiet rocky pools
On a beach not far away,
Secretively bubbling
A crab comes out to play.

The sand is softly sliding down
His sandy yellow shell,
And little eyes on stalks peer round
To see if all is well.

He sidles out along the beach
Where waves are rushing in
And holds aloft his fiddler's claw
For the concert to begin.

The prawns and shrimps begin the tune
The limpets harmonise;
The crab begins his solo piece
With gently waving eyes.

In thundering tones the waves crash in
To swell the symphony,
Then whelks and cockles softly sing
And modulate the key.

The fiddler crab takes up the strain
The crescendo now is heard
The music lifts, then dies away
To end on a minor third.

With pride and dignity, the crab
Now bows to great applause
And then returns, as if to say,
"There will be no encores."

Once more the pools are silent
The crab is seen no more
The cry of gulls and the murmuring sea
Are the only sounds of the shore.

Rhinoceros

An elephantine tank comes rumbling thru' the glade
The bulk of a rhinoceros emerges from the shade.
He glares around him grimly with little red rimmed eyes,
"What creature dares come near me?" that rhino boldly cries.
But as he roars his challenge, just spoiling for a match,
He feels an itch upon his back, and how he wants to scratch!
"Oh scratch my back, or I'll go mad!" rhinoceros he cried.
"Just hold still, and I'll oblige," a tick-bird then replied.
And of that nasty itching tick the birdie made an end,
Now the rhino has the tick-bird as his one and only friend.

Hummingbird

Hummingbirds, bedecked in colours wonderful and bright
Are jewels of the Americas, they're miracles in flight.
They are alive with energy, and scientists have reckoned
That hummingbirds can beat their wings at fifty times a second!
Maybe at a flowering bush in sunny Ecuador
Or feeders in a garden in the state of Arkansas
Any place where sweetness can be found this bird will come
You'll see a flash of colour, and the tiny wings will hum
Darting to each blossom with his long and slender bill
Sipping at the nectar till at last he's had his fill
He hovers, then flies in reverse or forwards, like a bee
Defending his domain from any rival he may see.
Beautiful and delicate, his beak a fragile stem
No larger than a baby's hand, an iridescent gem.

Penguin

Slipping, sliding on the ice
Comical waddle on the rocks
Pudgy, awkward old man penguin
With embarrassing orange socks.

Flippers flapping, all ungainly
Hardy dignifies a bird!
Humboldt's, King or cute Adelie
Seen on land seem quite absurd.

But then see them in the water
Diving with courageous flair:
Fishing experts, sleek and agile
Flying as if through the air.

Hippopotamus

A roil of mud and water
Amid the turmoil a head
Rises
Beneath two bead-black eyes
A gap appears
Spreads, seems to split the head.
Behind ivory mountains
A red carpet-tongue disappears
Down a bottomless chasm
While the split widens, widens...
Slowly the gaping hole
Contracts, while the great grey head
Slides back into the great grey water
And peace.
But a moment has passed
The hippopotamus has yawned.

Aardvark

There was I doing no harm,
Scratching about with my termite mates,
When suddenly, there were sounds of alarm
Followed by the sound every termite hates
        That grotty old Aardvark grubbing at our nest!
        If he was vegetarian, perhaps we'd get some rest!

We build our towers metres high
In an effort to make them aardvark proof
The next thing you know, we're exposed to the sky
For that earth pig has knocked off our roof!
        The ground begins to rumble, the earth begins to shake
        All my knees were knocking, and my head began to ache!

The walls were dug out by a mighty claw
And a long sticky tongue shot out of the snout;
A flick and a lick, and my friends were no more
For they had gone in where that tongue had come out!
        When the aardvark left us, I was shaken and inert
        I suppose I should be grateful, as I could have been dessert!

I packed up my bags and I ran and I ran
The ground isn't safe for termites like me.
If aardvarks can't climb [and I don't think they can],
I'm making my home at the top of a tree.

Otter

As the sunlight splashes diamonds on the rushing river's flow
A lithe and lissom body glides where reeds and rushes grow.
With bright black eyes and glistening fur, the otter makes no sound
But dips beneath the water where his next meal may be found.
And though the fishes dart and leap, it's clear they've met their match;
There's no doubt who's the winner when the otter's playing "Catch!"
And when his belly's full of fish, the otter just has fun.
His playground is the river where he romps 'til day is done.

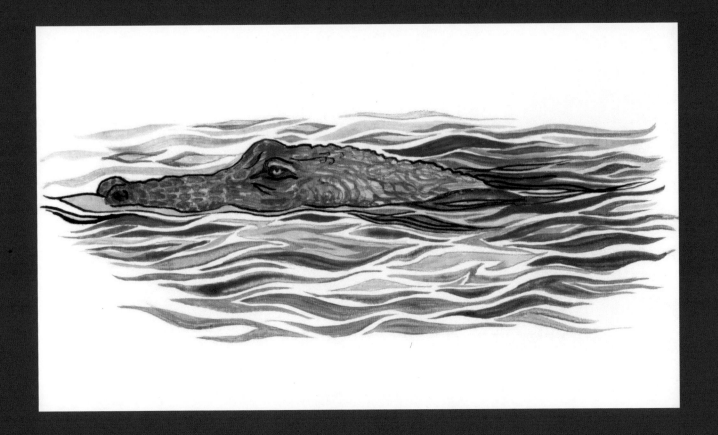

Alligator

"But what do alligators eat?"

The insistent voice said.

"Hush not so loud

Or you'll go straight to bed!"

"But there's nobody near us

And it pleases me so

To ask lots of questions

Why should I speak low?"

A snap! And a soft little swish

Chuckles, "Now do you know?!"

Printed in Great Britain
by Amazon